Bygone Surrey

Kevin McCormack

Ian Allan
PUBLISHING

Front cover: In October 1965, against a backdrop of Reigate Hill, RT3190, an example of LT's first standard postwar double-deck bus type, prepares to climb Cockshot Hill after passing the former East Surrey Traction Co's bus garage (with the red roof tiles) in Bell Street and adjacent offices (the multi-gabled building on the corner of Lesbourne Road). *Roy Hobbs*

Back cover: The photographer unexpectedly got two for the price of one when he waited for a trolleybus to appear on Kingston Bridge to enhance this view of the River Thames. The date is April 1962, at which time the last of these vehicles were about to be withdrawn. *Marcus Eavis / Online Transport Archive*

Previous page: A Redhill–Reading train hauled by Class N 2-6-0 No 31814 calls at Betchworth on 4 July 1964. Steam would be replaced by diesel traction in January 1966. If anything, the station looks better today, and the original spiral lamp posts now carry replica gas lights. *Neil Davenport*

Left: Abandoning his horse-drawn golden carriage, for his annual visit to present prizes at City of London Freemen's School in Ashtead Park the Lord Mayor of London travels instead by Rolls-Royce, seen here outside the school's Main House (formerly Ashtead Park House), most of which dates back to 1792. *Author*

First published 2009

ISBN 978 0 7110 3337 5

Published by Ian Allan Publishing

an imprint of Ian Allan Publishing Ltd, Hersham, Surrey KT12 4RG
Printed in England by Ian Allan Printing Ltd, Hersham, Surrey KT12 4RG

Code: 0907/B

Visit the Ian Allan Publishing website at www.ianallanpublishing.com

Introduction

Bygone Surrey is my third transport-themed general colour album showing how everyday life and familiar places have changed over the last 30-60 years. I have covered the area where I was brought up (*Bygone London*) and my birthplace (*Bygone Edinburgh*), so it was perhaps only a matter of time before I tackled the county in which I have now been living for more than 30 years.

In many people's minds Surrey epitomises the stockbroker belt — an affluent and mainly rural area with little industry and plenty of horses. This perspective is largely true, particularly following the transfer in 1965, for administrative purposes, of the north-eastern corner to Greater London. Mention of the county today conjures up images of the North Downs, the large areas of outstanding beauty open to the public and the pretty villages dotted all around. Indeed, there cannot be many counties that boast of having a thatched bus shelter (at Westcott on the A25)!

In terms of transport, since World War 2 the most noticeable change has probably been to the county's bus services. From its creation in 1933 through to 1969 London Transport ('LT') was responsible for most of these, other than in the westernmost parts, where the Aldershot & District Traction Co ('A&D')

held sway. On 1 January 1970 LT's Country Area bus and Green Line coach services were transferred to a new company, London Country Bus Services ('LCBS'). This company inherited a largely aged fleet against the background of increasing car ownership, making many rural services uneconomic even with one-person operation (*i.e.* without conductors). Privatisation of bus services has brought about an improvement in overall standards but at the price of a much-reduced bus network — and the livery of the vehicles, often garish, just doesn't look right against a green and pleasant landscape!

As regards railways, Surrey was served by the Southern Railway (formed in 1923 as an amalgamation of three large railway companies — the London and South Western, the London, Brighton & South Coast and the South Eastern & Chatham) and then, from nationalisation in 1948 until privatisation in the 1990s, by the Southern Region of British Railways. Much of the suburban network and most of the main lines had been electrified prior to World War 2, and the remaining scheduled steam workings ceased in 1967, although steam survives on some special trains. Surrey survived the notorious Beeching axe of the early 1960s relatively unscathed, losing only the Guildford–Horsham line.

A posse of Hales and McCormacks (spot the author!) decorate Coxes Lock on the Wey Navigation at Ham Moor, near Addlestone, in May 1985. In the background is the magnificent iron mill of 1776, which closed in 1983 and has now been converted into apartments. This canal section of the River Wey, now owned by the National Trust, opened to barge traffic in 1653 as a link to the River Thames and the Port of London.
George Hale

The county has many bridleways and some well-known racecourses (Epsom Downs, Sandown Park, Kempton Park and Lingfield Park), and horse riding is very much part of the Surrey scene. Indeed, the Derby, held at Epsom Downs in early June, is one of the most famous horse races in the world. Two other forms of transport in Surrey, significant in terms of leisure pursuits, which are represented in this book are private flying, from aerodromes such as Fairoaks and Redhill, and boating along inland waterways.

The various alterations to Surrey's administrative boundaries over the years have complicated the geographical scope of this book. For example, in 1965 Surrey lost towns such as Croydon, Sutton, Kingston and Richmond but gained Staines (Spelthorne). Gatwick Airport was transferred to West Sussex in 1974. However, the areas that have moved from Surrey into Greater London, which ironically include the County Council Offices in Kingston, retain 'Surrey' as part of their postal addresses! Nevertheless, I have disregarded this aspect and have based my criterion for picture coverage on whether the location in question was administered by Surrey County Council *at the time of the photograph*; as a result I am able to feature a wider range of transport, including trolleybuses and airliners. Wherever possible the photographs are of identifiable locations, for the benefit not only of bus and railway enthusiasts but of anyone interested in seeing how transport and, indeed, his/her local area has changed over the years.

A few photographs are my own, but the remainder were taken by various fellow transport enthusiasts, to whom I am most grateful — Roy Hobbs, Peter Trevaskis, Neil Davenport, Mike Harries, Michael Furnell, Chris Evans, Bruce Jenkins, Peter Gascoine, John May, Mike Hudson, Bob Bridger and Geoff Rixon. Photographs by Marcus Eavis and Martin Jenkins are reproduced courtesy of the Online Transport Archive, and those by Frank Hunt courtesy of the Light Railway Transit Association. Thanks are due also for the assistance provided by Les Smith, Roger Jones, John May, Janice Edwards and the Aldershot & District Bus Interest Group.

On 1 September 1968 the much-lamented 'Brighton Belle' electric Pullman train, introduced upon electrification of the Brighton line in 1933, approaches Earlswood travelling south, having taken the Quarry line, which was created to by-pass congestion at Redhill station. A yellow panel already covers the Pullman coat of arms, and the train will soon lose its traditional livery in favour of British Rail corporate blue and grey. *R. Copson / Online Transport Archive*

The pictures in the main body of the book fan out approximately north, west, south and east from Leatherhead, which is roughly in the centre of the area of coverage, and end up with nearby Epsom and Ashtead. The range of locations featured has been limited by the availability of suitable nostalgic and, preferably, unpublished material, so inevitably there are some omissions; any readers hoping to find a bygone view of Clacket Lane Services on the M25 will be sadly disappointed! Nevertheless, there should be sufficient variety in these pages to give a flavour of the Surrey many of us remember.

Kevin R. McCormack
Ashtead, Surrey
May 2009

When the author was growing up in West London one of his local bus routes was the 65 service from Ealing (Argyle Road) to Leatherhead (an unknown, very distant place!). The service was later shortened, and the southern section from Kingston taken over by route 71 depicted here (now partly covered by route 465). RT4286 joins a traffic queue in North Street, Leatherhead, before terminating at the bus garage in Guildford Road.

Martin Jenkins / Online Transport Archive

Above: Located beside the railway bridge, diagonally opposite the entrance to the Leisure Centre, Leatherhead bus garage has suffered the same fate as almost all former LT Country Area bus garages and has been demolished. In this view dating from August 1977 RT1139 lays over before returning to Richmond, while a former Green Line coach, modernised RF79, has just returned from Headley Court, Pebblecombe and Box Hill (Greenacres) on route 416. *Mike Harries*

Right: Wild animals are what most people associated with Chessington Zoo (now Chessington World of Adventures), but how many readers remember the old LT tramcar and stage coach, photographed here on 20 April 1957, that used to stand in the grounds near the bus terminus? London bade farewell to its trams in 1952 (until they returned to the Croydon area in 2000), but the example in this view, No 1858, was saved and can nowadays be found at the East Anglia Transport Museum at Carlton Colville. *Neil Davenport*

Left: The severe weather of December 1962/January 1963 caused the River Thames to freeze over, an occurrence almost unprecedented in modern times. This view depicts Hampton Court Bridge from the East Molesey side, with the Palace visible in the background above the bridge. *Geoff Rixon*

Above: On a warm summer's day — 13 June 1976 — one of the legendary Salter's steamers, *Empress of India*, pulls away from Hampton Court Pier (the Palace is behind the trees). The vessel was built in 1898 but was broken up a few years ago. *Marcus Eavis / Online Transport Archive*

Above: London had the largest trolleybus system in the world, operations commencing in the Kingston area in 1931 and ending there in May 1962. At a location that will be familiar to many, 'L3' trolleybus No 1431 and RF405 compete to be the first to reach Kingston Bridge during the final days of trolleybus operation. *Marcus Eavis / Online Transport Archive*

Right: Featuring a policeman controlling the pedestrian crossing, this view along Clarence Street in the direction of Kingston Bridge serves as a reminder of just how busy was the centre of Kingston-upon-Thames before this section was pedestrianised. The photograph was taken in early 1962, a few weeks before trolleybus operation came to an end. *Marcus Eavis / Online Transport Archive*

Before the advent of the full-fronted, underfloor-engined RF class, LT's early-postwar single-decker buses were based on prewar designs. Photographed in 1959, TD106, a Leyland Tiger with Mann Egerton bodywork, looks archaic as it grinds along Clarence Street, Kingston, before passing C&A's department store at the junction with London Road. The bus is operating a 219 service to Weybridge station. *Marcus Eavis / Online Transport Archive*

LT's standard single-deck bus and Green Line coach, introduced in the early 1950s, was the RF, of which no fewer than 700 were ultimately delivered. The last survivors operated routes 218 and 219 from Kingston garage until the end of March 1979, RF481 being seen at Esher during the final week of RF operation.

Apart from the vehicle and the combined bus/Green Line coach stop little has changed over the ensuing 30 years; the wooden bus shelter remains, and — perhaps more surprisingly — so does the cinema (extending behind the shops, with its frontage behind the middle tree). *Roy Hobbs*

Viewed from Richmond Bridge, with the railway bridge in the background, the pleasure boat *Kingswood*, built in 1915, has just passed Corporation Island as it heads for Twickenham and Kingston. The *Kingswood* still operates today on this part of the River Thames.
Marcus Eavis / Online Transport Archive

14

A venerable electric train dating from 1914, on its way from Broad Street to Richmond, leaves Kew Gardens station in 1957. The station building, dating from the line's opening in 1869, is Listed, as is the reinforced-concrete footbridge, designed by French engineer François Hennebique and built in 1912, its high sides intended to protect passengers' clothing from the smoke of steam locomotives. *Marcus Eavis / Online Transport Archive*

Walton-on-Thames railway station was linked to the town centre by a bus service introduced in 1923 by the Walton-on-Thames Motor Co Ltd, which latterly used Bedford OB buses. This one, built in 1948, is seen outside the station in August 1969. The company was taken over in 1970 by Golden Miller, which extended the service and numbered it 604, but this did not last long, and subsequently LT route 218 was diverted to serve the station. *Martin Jenkins / Online Transport Archive*

The last scheduled steam-hauled service into Waterloo — indeed, into London — approaches Weybridge in the early evening of 9 July 1967 in the capable hands of rebuilt Bulleid 'Merchant Navy' Pacific No 35030 *Elder-Dempster Lines*; the Bournemouth-line electric service would commence the following day. The end of London-area steam was of such significance that the author succeeded in persuading his ambivalent parents to witness this tragic event with him! *Author*

Above: The 27-year lifespan of LT's RF-type buses was due partly to accommodation problems at Kingston garage, their replacements being considerably larger (with a carrying capacity of 63 as against the RFs' 39), enabling frequencies to be reduced. This RF is seen in Shepperton Road, Laleham, on a 218 journey from Staines to Kingston. *Martin Jenkins / Online Transport Archive*

Right: Before the advent of low-floor buses and with severe length restrictions precluding the use of long single-deckers, the only suitable buses for busy routes with low bridges were 'lowbridge' double-deckers, which achieved their low height by means of inconvenient four-abreast seating upstairs and a sunken offside gangway that protruded into the lower deck. One such vehicle, RLH20, on its way from Staines in August 1964, has stopped just beyond the Duke's Head, Addlestone. The public house, along with the shop with the protective blinds, has vanished. *Peter Gascoine*

Left: The Englefield Green area was one of the last bastions of gas lighting, still very much in evidence in this July 1974 view. A few, converted to electricity, still remain near the green, which RT4046 is passing as it heads for Staines on the long 441 route from High Wycombe; the author's 1932 Austin 7 can be seen hiding in the background. There were nearly 7,000 buses of the RT family, built between 1939 and 1954, and the last survivors remained in public service until 1979. *Author*

Above: Flying through the air with the greatest of ease, a daring young lady rides on the top wing of a Tiger Moth biplane at the 1964 Air Display at Fairoaks Aerodrome, located between Ottershaw and Chobham. *Author*

Left and below left: Until its merger in 1972 with Thames Valley (following which it traded as Alder Valley) Aldershot & District was the principal operator connecting with LT's westerly bus-service boundaries in Surrey, at places such as Chertsey, Woking and Guildford, as well as operating to the west of the county and providing an express coach service into London. Like that of LT's Country Area buses its livery — two shades of green relieved by cream — blended well with the Surrey countryside. In the first picture, dating from 5 November 1961, No 335, a Weymann-bodied AEC Reliance built in 1958, passes the Church of St John the Baptist in Church Road, Windlesham, *en route* for Woking, while in the second, taken in May 1960, a postwar Dennis Lancet lays over alongside Chobham war memorial, with Cannon Cottage (*c*1630) and Laurel Cottage in the background. *Peter Trevaskis (both)*

Right: When the author took this picture of an engineering train resting at Tunnel Hill, between Brookwood and Ash Vale, while on a school cadet-force outing to the nearby shooting ranges in summer 1965, he did not appreciate the notoriety of the locomotive. Originally No A800 *River Cray*, one of a class of 2-6-4 tank engines, it derailed at Sevenoaks in 1927 while hauling an express train, the accident claiming 13 lives and highlighting the instability of these locomotives at high speed, with the result that all were rebuilt as 2-6-0 tender engines. *Author*

Left: For its more rural bus routes along narrow lanes A&D used Dennis Falcons. These were light and manœuvrable vehicles but were excessively noisy and consequently unpopular with passengers. No 244, dating from 1954, is depicted at the Woking terminus alongside the railway line, evidenced by the disappearing Waterloo-bound electric unit on the left of the picture. *John May*

Below: The erstwhile Southern Railway was a great exponent of concrete, having its own manufacturing facility, and Woking station, pictured here on 11 March 1967, typifies the use of this material. Still fitted with its original 'air-smoothed' casing, unrebuilt Bulleid 'Battle of Britain' Pacific No 34057 *Biggin Hill* has just arrived with the 12.39pm Waterloo–Basingstoke train. *Bob Bridger*

Above: A&D Dennis Lancet J3 No 115 pauses at the stop outside the Rose and Thistle at Frimley Green on its way from Woking to Aldershot in 1959. The vehicle, following an early-1930s design, was actually built in 1949, and the last survivors of its type were not withdrawn from service until 1961. *Peter Trevaskis*

Right: Covering part of Guildford–Aldershot service 20 as an extra vehicle in 1959, Dennis Lance No 215 stands at the War Memorial in Hunts Hill Road, Normandy, ready to take up its morning rush-hour duty. Dating from 1954, this East Lancs-bodied vehicle was one of A&D's first 8ft-wide double-deckers, the extra width being denoted by the white steering wheel fitted as a reminder to drivers. *Peter Trevaskis*

Left: A&D Dennis Lancet J3 No 114,
built in 1949, stands in Castle Street,
Farnham, on service 17 to Grayscott
(Fox & Pelican) via Tilford. In 1961
this handsome vehicle suffered the
indignity of being cut down and
converted into a towing lorry.
Peter Trevaskis

Right: The last traditional-looking
A&D Dennis Lancets were the J10s,
which were built in 1950 to the new,
increased maximum dimensions for
buses of 8ft width and 30ft length.
One such vehicle is seen here on
25 August 1959 passing the war
memorial at Seale, against the
charming backdrop of St Lawrence's
Church and the Hog's Back.
Peter Trevaskis

Right: A&D was a firm supporter of
Dennis vehicles, which were built
locally at Guildford, but eschewed
this manufacturer's full-fronted,
underfloor-engined single-deckers,
preferring AEC Reliances. One of the
latter, Weymann-bodied No 372,
dating from 1960, is pictured in
Malthouse Lane, Hambledon, at the
junction with Woodlands Road,
in March 1961. *Peter Trevaskis*

Above: In the early 1950s Bristol developed a new design for low-height double-decker buses, based on the concept of a drop-centre rear axle which allowed a sunken gangway on the lower deck; this in turn permitted a reduction in the height of the ceiling/upper-deck floor and thus eliminated the need for inconvenient four-abreast seating and sunken offside gangway of the traditional 'lowbridge' design. Dennis's version of the Bristol Lodekka was the Loline, and in this view A&D No 353, an East Lancs-bodied Loline dating from 1958, is standing outside the company's booking office/waiting room on the A3 at Hindhead. *John May*

Right: The prettiest station on the Guildford–Horsham line, which closed on 14 June 1965, four months short of its centenary, was Baynards (initially called Little Vachery). Situated in an isolated location on a track leading to the Baynards Estate, the impressive station is now privately owned and has been lovingly restored. The flowers were blooming well on 10 October 1953 in this view towards nearby Sussex. *Neil Davenport*

Left and above: Although much of the defunct Guildford–Horsham line has been turned into a footpath there is no sign of the railway's ever having entered the centre of Cranleigh, where these two photographs were taken on 22 May 1965. In the first,

Ivatt '2MT' 2-6-2T No 41301 calls with a train for Horsham. The photographer would now be standing in the service road for Stocklund Square's maisonettes and shops and Sainsbury's in the High Street. *Marcus Eavis / Online Transport Archive (both)*

Left: In contrast with Cranleigh, there remains plenty of evidence of the Guildford–Horsham-line railway station at Bramley & Wonersh, seen here in April 1965. Although only a tiny corner of the station house remains — on account of a King Edward VII postbox (still in use) embedded therein — the platforms and station signs are still extant, and replica level-crossing gates and a close imitation of the small shelter shown here have been installed.
Neil Davenport

Above right: Headed by an Ivatt 2-6-2 tank running bunker-first, a train from Horsham has just emerged from St Catherine's Hill and is about to enter Guildford station in June 1965. The locomotive shed is now long gone, the site being occupied by the tiered Farnham Road multi-storey car park.
Marcus Eavis / Online Transport Archive

Right: Chilworth & Albury station, on the Reading–Redhill line, looks smarter today than it does in this view of a Reading-bound train headed by Class N 2-6-0 No 31862. The photograph was taken on 3 January 1965, the last day of steam operation on these services. *Marcus Eavis / Online Transport Archive*

Because of the confined space occupied by Guildford engine shed, coaling facilities and ash pits were located elsewhere — directly opposite, but screened off from the station! The platforms and long footbridge act as a marker in this picture of Class N No 31408, taken in June 1965. *Author*

Guildford station, as rebuilt in 1880, is heaving with railway
enthusiasts in this view of preserved Class T9 No 120, as it makes
a photographic stop while hauling a Locomotive Club of Great
Britain railtour on 24 June 1962. The station would be rebuilt
again in 1987, but the old footbridge remains. *Mike Hudson*

Class U 2-6-0 No 31615 approaches Guildford station with a train from Reading in 1959. Most of the greenery has since given way to modern, mainly commercial development, and the only recognisable feature today is the building right of centre, between the Portsmouth line from Waterloo via Woking and the local line from Waterloo via Cobham or Epsom. *Marcus Eavis / Online Transport Archive*

An ex-LT Guy Special (GS) operated by Tillingbourne Valley Services passes an A&D Dennis Loline III/Alexander at Guilford's Farnham Road bus station. This latter, on a site now used as a surface car park, was in the shadow of St Nicolas' Church, between the George Abbot public house (named after a local boy who became Archbishop of Canterbury in 1610) and Town Wharf, on the River Wey. The buildings in the distance on the right are across the river, beyond the 1960s Friary Bridge, and form the rear of Rodboro Buildings, which is now occupied by the Academy of Contemporary Music. Early in the 20th century these buildings were used as a factory by Dennis for building vehicles and used to flank the north side of Onslow Street bus station (see overleaf). *Marcus Eavis / Online Transport Archive*

Left: A brand-new AEC Reliance/Willowbrook of Safeguard Coaches pulls out of Guildford's Onslow Street bus station in July 1964. Safeguard, a family-run business established in 1924, is still going strong, but much has changed at the lower end of the town, this location being completely unrecognisable today. *Bruce Jenkins*

Right: Pictured in front of the riverside Electric Works, dating from 1913 (and nowadays the extended Electric Theatre), a lowbridge LT Regent, RLH11, prepares to depart Onslow Street bus station in December 1965. Also visible are an RT and, on the right, a Tillingbourne Valley ex-LT Guy Special (GS). *Robin Hannay collection*

Right: Fame at last for the girl with the 1960s beehive hairstyle! The location is the top of North Street, Guildford, with the former Horse & Groom public house (wrecked by terrorists in 1974, rebuilt and now a shop) on the right, next to the clock tower standing atop the public lavatories (dating from 1874 and originally the fire station). The bus is A&D No 124, an East Lancs-bodied Dennis Lance K3 of 1949. *Martin Jenkins / Online Transport Archive*

Above: Although there are still some wooden bus shelters along this stretch of the A25 leading into Guildford (even fitted with electronic timetables!) this one at Merrow has succumbed to road widening. The Parish Church of St John the Evangelist and another Horse & Groom public house provide the backdrop for this early-1960s view of Tillingbourne Valley Bedford OB EUX 7, built in 1949. *Martin Jenkins / Online Transport Archive*

Right: Bound for Guildford, Guy Special GS36 pauses opposite the Bull's Head in The Street, Ewhurst, on 7 August 1964. This unusual instance of an LT bus using a 'provincial' bus stop would cease four days later, for London Transport, which operated route 448 jointly with Tillingbourne Valley, was about to withdraw from this arrangement. *Peter Gascoine*

Left: Fast forward nearly 30 years! In the 1950s and '60s LT used 26-seat Guy Specials for routes along the narrow lanes around the North Downs between Guildford and Dorking, and in the 1980s and early 1990s some of these were re-created on summer Sundays as Ramblers' and Surrey Hills leisure services, using appropriate vintage buses. In this view, dating from the summer of 1993, GS13 pauses at the pretty village of Holmbury St Mary, previously called Felday and renamed in 1879 in recognition of nearby Holmbury Hill and the newly built St Mary's Church (partly visible on the right). *Author*

Above: Passing a site now occupied by Mole Valley District Council's Pippbrook offices, demoted Green Line coach RF159 pauses in Reigate Road, Dorking, in May 1971, on route 439 to Goodwyns Farm Estate and Brockham. This vehicle was one of 175 RF coaches re-styled in the mid-1960s to update the Green Line image, the work including the fitting of twin headlights and the application of a broad waistband, originally pale green (see overleaf). However, their heyday was short-lived, more-modern-looking coaches being introduced in a vain attempt to stem the decline in patronage of these largely cross-London services. *Mike Harries*

Viewed from the photographer's house in October 1968, RF54, in full Green Line livery complete with roof-mounted route boards, speeds along London Road (A24), Dorking, on service 714 from Luton via Oxford Circus. It is passing the goods yard at Dorking station, beyond which is the substantial station building, destined to be replaced by something nasty in the early 1980s. Magnificent Box Hill rises up behind. *Mike Harries*

This view north at Dorking station dates from June 1963 and, indeed, could have been recorded only in mid-summer, for it depicts the 5.13am London Bridge–Brighton newspaper train, which also carried passengers; the locomotive is rebuilt 'West Country' Pacific No 34014 *Budleigh Salterton*. Electric trains to Dorking were introduced in 1925, and this unusual early-morning service was the final scheduled steam-hauled passenger working on this line, destined to be withdrawn a few months after the photograph was taken. *Roy Hobbs*

Left: Having turned off the A24 south of Dorking, former Green Line coach RCL2260 passes Holmwood Common on 4 August 1977. Times, as well as buses, have changed — the white building on the left becoming a tattoo parlour! *Michael Furnell*

Above: From time to time LT's Country Bus & Coach Department found itself short of green buses and had to borrow red exampes from the Central Area. One such period of need spanned the LCBS takeover of 'green' services on 1 January 1970, RF374 being seen the following August at Strood Green (Tyndale Road) on a short-working of Dorking–Redhill route 439. This location remains virtually unchanged today; even the post box in the background (right) survives, although a house extension has taken the place of the telephone box. *Roy Hobbs*

Located in Surrey until 1974, when a change to the county boundary saw it transferred to West Sussex, Gatwick was once known for its racecourse — from 1916 to 1918 the Grand National was held there — with its own railway station. However, 1934 saw the opening of the commercial airport, which has been growing ever since, and today it is Britain's second-busiest. This view, dating from 22 July 1966, shows passengers disembarking from a Douglas DC-3 (Dakota) airliner of Dan-Air Services. *Marcus Eavis / Online Transport Archive*

An ex-Great Western Railway engine operating in Surrey! For route familiarisation, two trains per day on the Southern Region's Reading–Redhill line were normally worked by Western Region crews who might be required to take summer excursion trains between the Midlands and the South Coast over this line.

This shot from June 1961 depicts the 6.50am from Reading (Southern) drawing into Reigate station behind '43xx' Mogul No 6385. As elsewhere, much here has changed, but surprisingly the period signalbox, an endangered species, remains in use.
Roy Hobbs

Left: A brand-new long Routemaster, RML2305, on loan to LT's Country Area from the Central Area, waits at the traffic lights in front of Reigate Old Town Hall (1728) on its way to Bromley North station in October 1965. This is now a one-way street, in the opposite direction. *Roy Hobbs*

Above: In June 1975 another long Routemaster, RML2312 (all the production Country Area Routemaster buses were built to the increased length of 30ft), waits in London Road, Reigate, with West Street behind. The bus shelter was one of the last remaining examples of this 1930s LT design and still stands today in reconstructed form. *Mike Harries*

Left: The head office of LT's Country Bus & Coach Department was in Lesbourne Road, Reigate, and since LT's inception in 1933 all routes through the town would normally have been operated by green buses. However, more vehicles loaned from the Central area are evident in this June 1967 photograph, taken at the end of Bell Street (before the introduction of the one-way system). RF438 is substituting for a green RF, while Leyland Atlantean XA29 is covering for a green Daimler Fleetline (XF) being used on comparative trials in the Central Area. *Roy Hobbs*

Left: An ex-Green Line Routemaster coach, RCL2260, passes through Horley on its way from Redhill to Crawley in the mid-1970s. LCBS would withdraw the last of its Routemasters in early 1980 following conversion of all its routes to one-person operation, almost the entire fleet being returned to LT. *John May*

Right: With the Plough Inn on the left and St John's Church in the background, RF677 heads along Church Road, Redhill, towards the junction with the A23 at Earlswood in October 1966. Route 430 from Reigate to Redhill, going 'round the houses', still operates, but the buses are painted two shades of blue. *Roy Hobbs*

Although the children appear to be taking a walk in the country as the village bus passes by, this is an optical illusion! In the background, on the southern outskirts of Redhill town centre, is the A23 Brighton Road, which ex-coach RCL2249 has just turned off in order to join Woodlands Road, Earlswood. The date is 4 August 1977. *Michael Furnell*

Those who have forgotten British Railways' attractive 1950s carmine-and-cream carriage livery are invited to savour the sight of this excursion train from the Western Region leaving Redhill station *en route* to the South Coast. Photographed on 7 May 1955, the locomotive, newly built Standard Class 4 2-6-0 No 76054, had just replaced an ex-Great Western Railway Mogul, which, because of clearance problems, would have been barred from proceeding beyond Redhill. *Neil Davenport*

Above: On 3 April 1965 a '6-PUL' electric unit, No 3015, approaches Quarry Tunnel on the Redhill-avoiding line. The '6-PUL' units, which included a Pullman car, were introduced in 1933 on the newly electrified Brighton line as superior trains to run alongside the luxurious 'Brighton Belle' (see page 4). *Jack Wyse*

Right: Another LT/LCBS garage that is now just a memory is Godstone, on the old A22, which was built by the East Surrey Traction Co (a predecessor of LT). RT4742, with a set of blinds belonging to another bus type, pauses outside the garage on a short-working of the West Croydon–Forest Row 409 service. *Michael Furnell*

Oxted station is on a line from London which later divides to serve either Uckfield or East Grinstead, both branches originally going to Lewes, the latter via a route which is now partly occupied by the preserved Bluebell Railway. Branching off the Uckfield line near Eridge was a spur to Tunbridge Wells West, and although this was subsequently closed part of its length is now occupied by the preserved Spa Valley Railway. Waiting to depart on 1 May 1962 are an evening commuter train from London Bridge to East Grinstead headed by BR Standard Class 4 2-6-4T No 80152 and an Oxted–Tunbridge Wells West push-and-pull train drawn by an ex-SECR 'H'-class 0-4-4T. *Mike Hudson*

Readers could be forgiven for thinking that this is a Southdown bus, particularly as it is in that company's livery and heading for Southdown territory. But no; in 1975 LCBS was suffering such an acute shortage of operational vehicles that it purchased three second-hand Leyland PD3s, placing them in service without even bothering to repaint them. LS3 was photographed on 5 September in Coulsdon Road, Caterham, on a 409 journey from West Croydon. *Chris Evans*

Left: As well as buying and borrowing old buses during its chronic vehicle shortage, LCBS surprised enthusiasts by recertifying four of its elderly RT buses for continued public service. Chelsham garage's RT3461 looks resplendent in its new National Bus Company livery, with all its body dents removed, as it leaves Warlingham Park Hospital on the evening of 24 May 1977. *Chris Evans*

Above: A De Havilland Heron similar to this one still graces the forecourt of Croydon Airport, although neither the aircraft nor the airport is operational. Most of the site has been built on, but some of the historic buildings on the A23 (Purley Way) still survive. This was the view northwest from the public enclosure in 1957, two years before the airport closed. *Marcus Eavis / Online Transport Archive*

Above: This is how East Croydon station and the surrounding area appeared on 1 March 1963 — nothing like it does today! The station has been rebuilt with an office block above, and the road outside is festooned with overhead wires and supporting structures serving the tram system introduced in 2000. *Mike Hudson*

Right: Wheels have now turned full circle. Trolleybuses replaced trams on the Crystal Palace–Sutton Green route in 1935/6 (and were themselves ousted by motor buses in March 1959), yet where 'B1' Leyland No 69 is standing — in Tamworth Road, with West Croydon station just out of sight to the left of the building in the background — trams now operate once more, albeit running in the opposite direction. *Frank Hunt*

By the time of their replacement by motor buses (on route 157) the 'B1' trolleybuses used on route 654 were the oldest in LT's fleet; they were also noteworthy through being fitted with a special braking system to cope with Anerley Hill's 1-in-9 gradient. This 1958 photograph was taken in Ringstead Road, Sutton, at the foot of which was No 89's home depot of Carshalton — a building which, surprisingly, still survives today. *Marcus Eavis / Online Transport Archive*

Sutton garage's RF485 waits opposite Tadworth station (identified by the overhanging gas lamp on the left) on its way from Tooting Broadway to Walton-on-the-Hill. Behind the bus is a half-red, half-green LT bus-stop flag topped by a red-and-green finial, indicating that it was served also by Green Line coaches (on route 727).
Martin Jenkins / Online Transport Archive

Left: The Fox at Lower Kingswood (on the right) now stands on the busy A217 dual-carriageway which takes vehicles to Junction 8 of the M25 at the top of Reigate Hill. In June 1969, before road widening, RF537 passes RC11 on Green Line service 727 (Gatwick Airport–Luton) prior to turning into Buckland Road at the end of its journey from Tooting Broadway on route 80. Delivered in 1965, RC11 was one of 14 powerful Willowbrook-bodied AEC Reliances which proved to be mechanically unreliable. *Roy Hobbs*

Above: It is perhaps difficult nowadays to imagine that traditional London double-decker buses once frequented Walton-on-the-Hill, but this is how it was in February 1967, when RT4374 was photographed working route 80A to Tooting Broadway. *Roy Hobbs*

Left: LT/LCBS buses of the RT family could be found throughout both the Central and Country areas. Tattenham Corner was one of those places where red and green RTs ran side by side, as evidenced by this photograph taken on 7 April 1975 at Great Tattenhams, opposite the railway station. With Epsom racecourse in the background, RT739 rests between journeys on route 164A while RT3137 pauses on a short-working of the 406, to Tadworth. *Michael Furnell*

Below: Epsom racecourse is served by two railway stations, and in this view (dating from 3 July 1955) the Epsom Downs terminus of the branch from Sutton still proudly proclaims allegiance to the pre-nationalisation Southern Railway. A housing estate now stands on this site, a new station building having been erected further back, nearer the Drift Bridge. *Neil Davenport*

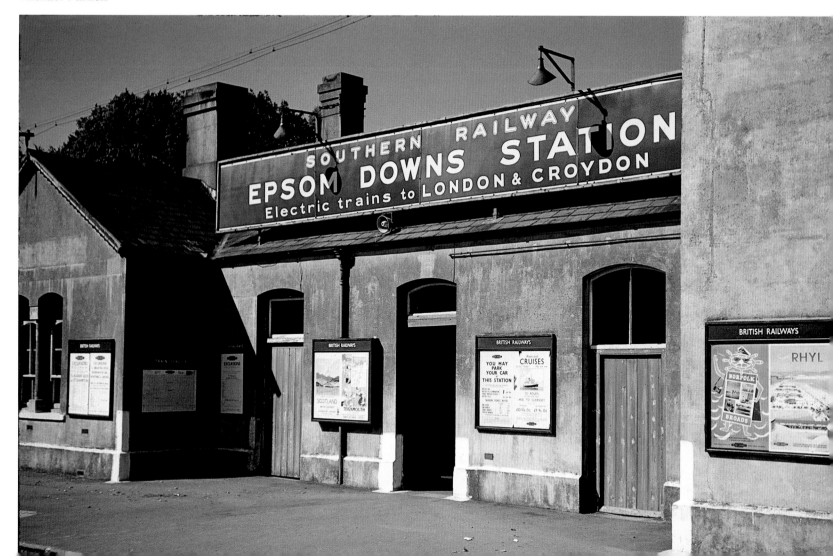

Above: The horses and riders have rounded Tattenham Corner and are sprinting along the finishing straight in the 1954 running of the Oaks — the fillies' equivalent of the Derby — on 4 June. The race was won by Sun Cap, ridden by Rae Johnstone.
Neil Davenport

Right: Moving on 10 years, a row of A&D Dennis Lances are lined up at the Derby at Epsom Downs as spectators take their seats in a temporary stand which looks as though it is reached by tall ladders! Its rudimentary features reflect less litigious times, when people took responsibility for their own personal safety.
Peter Gascoine

Left: No safety helmet or high-visibility jacket for this policeman atop his handsome steed at the 1954 Oaks meeting at Epsom Downs. The racecourse has undergone extensive modernisation over recent years, although the building on the right, which is close to today's Queen's Stand, has survived. The Oaks is one of the five British Classic races and was first run in 1779, a year before the first Derby. Both races were established by the Earl of Derby, the Oaks taking its name from his estate at Carshalton. *Neil Davenport*

Right: Litter left behind on race days at Epsom Downs is clearly not a modern-day phenomenon, as this view, recorded on the same day as the previous picture, clearly illustrates. *Neil Davenport*

Left: Definitely not preparing for the Oaks or the Derby, these riders are making their way along Waterloo Road, Epsom, close to the main railway station, in May 1969. They are about to cross the High Street into Ashley Road, presumably heading for the Downs. *Neil Davenport*

Above: On 30 September 1967 the Mayor of Epsom had the honour of opening the new refuse-disposal plant in Blenheim Road. As His Worship (right) discharges his responsibilities the Mayoral Rolls-Royce stands ready to whisk him away. *Neil Davenport*

Left: Epsom town centre, viewed from the west end of the High Street on 19 April 1949. This stretch of road is now one-way, the carriageway on the right being pedestrianised and frequently occupied by market stalls. Although the cinema has been demolished most of the buildings beyond survive, including, of course, the clock tower dating from 1854. *Neil Davenport*

Above: The final two photographs in the book feature the author's village, Ashtead, midway between Epsom and Leatherhead. On this particular day in the winter of 1981/2 the author's local shops, Craddocks Parade, are receiving a visit from a pony and trap, serving as a reminder that this was the normal means of transport locally before the advent of the motor car. *Author*

In Barnett Wood Lane, a stone's throw from Craddocks Parade, is Ashtead Pond, where in August 1978 a family of swans is waiting patiently for a bus on route 418 (nowadays 479) to Bookham! Note that despite the passage of eight years since LT ceased to operate this service the bus-stop flags bearing the famous bullseye motif had yet to be replaced. *Author*